50 Wholesome Dinners for the Whole Family

By: Kelly Johnson

Table of Contents

- Classic Meatloaf with Mashed Potatoes
- Baked Lemon Garlic Salmon
- Chicken and Vegetable Stir-Fry
- Spaghetti with Turkey Meatballs
- One-Pot Chicken Alfredo
- Beef and Bean Chili
- Homemade Chicken Tacos
- Roasted Chicken with Root Vegetables
- Vegetable and Quinoa Stir-Fry
- Baked Ziti with Spinach and Ricotta
- Grilled Chicken with Sweet Potato Fries
- Broccoli and Cheddar Stuffed Chicken
- Veggie-Packed Shepherd's Pie
- Grilled Salmon with Brown Rice
- Beef and Vegetable Skillet
- Sweet and Sour Chicken with Rice
- Shrimp and Vegetable Skewers
- Veggie and Bean Burrito Bowls
- Slow-Cooker Chicken Stew
- Teriyaki Chicken with Steamed Rice
- Beef Tacos with Fresh Salsa
- Turkey and Sweet Potato Chili
- Creamy Vegetable Soup with Whole Wheat Croutons
- Grilled Pork Chops with Apple Slaw
- Lemon Herb Chicken with Quinoa
- Baked Salmon with Avocado Salsa
- Roasted Veggie Buddha Bowls
- Spaghetti Squash Primavera
- Chicken Fajitas with Peppers and Onions
- Mediterranean Chicken with Hummus and Veggies
- Beef and Sweet Potato Stir-Fry
- Veggie-Loaded Pasta Primavera
- Chicken and Broccoli Casserole
- Grilled Steak with Mashed Cauliflower
- Veggie-Packed Baked Mac and Cheese

- Slow-Cooker Beef and Vegetable Soup
- Fish Tacos with Mango Salsa
- One-Pan Baked Chicken and Veggies
- Roasted Turkey with Cranberry Sauce
- Pesto Chicken and Zucchini Noodles
- Eggplant Parmesan with Spaghetti
- BBQ Chicken with Roasted Potatoes
- Sweet Potato and Black Bean Enchiladas
- Grilled Chicken Caesar Salad
- Baked Falafel with Couscous
- Stuffed Bell Peppers with Brown Rice
- Turkey Burgers with Avocado
- Beef and Barley Soup
- Shrimp Scampi with Whole Wheat Pasta
- Chicken and Spinach Quesadillas

Classic Meatloaf with Mashed Potatoes

Ingredients:

- **For the Meatloaf:**
    - 1 lb ground beef
    - 1/2 lb ground pork
    - 1/2 cup breadcrumbs
    - 1/4 cup milk
    - 1/4 cup ketchup
    - 1 small onion, finely chopped
    - 1 egg
    - 1 tsp garlic powder
    - 1 tsp salt
    - 1/2 tsp black pepper
    - 1 tbsp Worcestershire sauce
    - 1/4 cup ketchup (for topping)
- **For the Mashed Potatoes:**
    - 4 large potatoes, peeled and cubed
    - 1/2 cup milk
    - 1/4 cup butter
    - Salt and pepper to taste

Instructions:

1. Preheat oven to 375°F (190°C).
2. In a large bowl, combine ground beef, ground pork, breadcrumbs, milk, ketchup, onion, egg, garlic powder, salt, pepper, and Worcestershire sauce. Mix until well combined.
3. Form the mixture into a loaf shape and place it on a baking sheet or in a loaf pan.
4. Spread 1/4 cup of ketchup on top of the meatloaf for glazing.
5. Bake for 50-60 minutes, or until the meatloaf reaches an internal temperature of 160°F (71°C).
6. Meanwhile, boil the potatoes in salted water for 15-20 minutes until tender. Drain and mash with milk, butter, salt, and pepper.
7. Serve the meatloaf with a side of mashed potatoes.

Baked Lemon Garlic Salmon

Ingredients:

- 4 salmon fillets
- 2 tbsp olive oil
- 2 tbsp lemon juice
- 3 garlic cloves, minced
- 1 tsp dried thyme
- Salt and pepper to taste
- Lemon wedges for serving

Instructions:

1. Preheat the oven to 400°F (200°C).
2. Place the salmon fillets on a baking sheet lined with parchment paper.
3. In a small bowl, mix olive oil, lemon juice, garlic, thyme, salt, and pepper.
4. Drizzle the lemon garlic mixture over the salmon fillets.
5. Bake for 12-15 minutes, or until the salmon is cooked through and flakes easily with a fork.
6. Serve with lemon wedges on the side.

Chicken and Vegetable Stir-Fry

Ingredients:

- 1 lb chicken breast, thinly sliced
- 1 tbsp soy sauce
- 1 tbsp hoisin sauce
- 1 tbsp oyster sauce
- 1 tbsp cornstarch
- 1 tbsp vegetable oil
- 1 bell pepper, sliced
- 1 zucchini, sliced
- 1 carrot, julienned
- 1/2 onion, sliced
- 2 garlic cloves, minced
- 1 tsp ginger, grated
- Cooked rice for serving

Instructions:

1. In a bowl, mix the chicken slices with soy sauce, hoisin sauce, oyster sauce, and cornstarch. Set aside.
2. Heat vegetable oil in a wok or large skillet over medium-high heat.
3. Add the chicken and stir-fry for 5-6 minutes, or until cooked through. Remove the chicken from the pan and set aside.
4. In the same pan, add the bell pepper, zucchini, carrot, and onion. Stir-fry for 3-4 minutes until tender-crisp.
5. Add garlic and ginger, and cook for an additional 1-2 minutes.
6. Return the chicken to the pan, stir to combine, and cook for another minute.
7. Serve the stir-fry over cooked rice.

Spaghetti with Turkey Meatballs

Ingredients:

- **For the Meatballs:**
    - 1 lb ground turkey
    - 1/2 cup breadcrumbs
    - 1/4 cup grated Parmesan cheese
    - 1 egg
    - 1/4 cup chopped parsley
    - 2 garlic cloves, minced
    - Salt and pepper to taste
- **For the Sauce:**
    - 1 can (28 oz) crushed tomatoes
    - 1 tbsp olive oil
    - 1 onion, chopped
    - 2 garlic cloves, minced
    - 1 tsp dried basil
    - 1 tsp dried oregano
    - Salt and pepper to taste
    - 8 oz spaghetti, cooked

Instructions:

1. Preheat oven to 375°F (190°C).
2. In a bowl, combine ground turkey, breadcrumbs, Parmesan, egg, parsley, garlic, salt, and pepper. Form the mixture into meatballs (about 1 inch in diameter) and place them on a baking sheet.
3. Bake the meatballs for 20-25 minutes, or until fully cooked.
4. In a separate pan, heat olive oil over medium heat. Sauté onion and garlic until softened, about 5 minutes.
5. Add crushed tomatoes, basil, oregano, salt, and pepper to the pan. Simmer for 10-15 minutes to let the flavors meld.
6. Add the cooked meatballs to the sauce and simmer for another 10 minutes.
7. Serve the meatballs and sauce over cooked spaghetti.

One-Pot Chicken Alfredo

Ingredients:

- 2 tbsp butter
- 1 lb chicken breast, cut into cubes
- 2 garlic cloves, minced
- 1 cup heavy cream
- 1 1/2 cups chicken broth
- 8 oz fettuccine pasta
- 1 cup grated Parmesan cheese
- Salt and pepper to taste
- Fresh parsley for garnish

Instructions:

1. Heat butter in a large skillet over medium heat. Add chicken and cook until browned and cooked through, about 6-7 minutes.
2. Add garlic and cook for another 1 minute.
3. Pour in heavy cream and chicken broth, bring to a simmer.
4. Add the fettuccine pasta and cook according to package instructions, stirring occasionally.
5. Once the pasta is cooked, stir in Parmesan cheese until the sauce thickens.
6. Season with salt and pepper to taste. Garnish with fresh parsley and serve.

Beef and Bean Chili

Ingredients:

- 1 lb ground beef
- 1 can kidney beans, drained and rinsed
- 1 can black beans, drained and rinsed
- 1 can diced tomatoes
- 1 onion, chopped
- 2 garlic cloves, minced
- 1 bell pepper, chopped
- 1 tbsp chili powder
- 1 tsp cumin
- Salt and pepper to taste

Instructions:

1. In a large pot, cook ground beef over medium heat until browned. Drain excess fat.
2. Add onion, garlic, and bell pepper, and cook for 5 minutes until softened.
3. Add chili powder, cumin, salt, pepper, kidney beans, black beans, and diced tomatoes. Stir to combine.
4. Simmer on low heat for 30-45 minutes, stirring occasionally.
5. Serve with your choice of toppings such as sour cream, cheese, and green onions.

Homemade Chicken Tacos

Ingredients:

- 1 lb chicken breast, cooked and shredded
- 1 packet taco seasoning
- 1/4 cup water
- 8 small taco shells
- Shredded lettuce
- Chopped tomatoes
- Shredded cheese
- Sour cream
- Salsa

Instructions:

1. In a skillet, heat shredded chicken with taco seasoning and water. Stir to combine and cook for 5-7 minutes.
2. Warm taco shells in the oven or microwave.
3. Assemble tacos by filling each shell with seasoned chicken, lettuce, tomatoes, cheese, sour cream, and salsa.
4. Serve immediately.

Roasted Chicken with Root Vegetables

Ingredients:

- 1 whole chicken (about 4 lbs)
- 2 tbsp olive oil
- 1 tsp rosemary
- 1 tsp thyme
- Salt and pepper to taste
- 4 large carrots, peeled and cut into chunks
- 3 potatoes, peeled and cut into chunks
- 2 onions, quartered

Instructions:

1. Preheat the oven to 425°F (220°C).
2. Rub the chicken with olive oil, rosemary, thyme, salt, and pepper. Place it in the center of a roasting pan.
3. Arrange the carrots, potatoes, and onions around the chicken.
4. Roast for 1 hour and 20 minutes, or until the chicken reaches an internal temperature of 165°F (75°C).
5. Let the chicken rest for 10 minutes before carving. Serve with the roasted vegetables.

Vegetable and Quinoa Stir-Fry

Ingredients:

- 1 cup quinoa
- 2 tbsp soy sauce
- 1 tbsp sesame oil
- 1 tbsp olive oil
- 1 zucchini, sliced
- 1 bell pepper, sliced
- 1 carrot, julienned
- 1/2 onion, chopped
- 1/2 cup frozen peas
- 2 garlic cloves, minced

Instructions:

1. Cook quinoa according to package instructions.
2. In a large skillet or wok, heat sesame oil and olive oil over medium heat. Add zucchini, bell pepper, carrot, and onion. Stir-fry for 4-5 minutes until tender-crisp.
3. Add garlic and frozen peas, and cook for another 2 minutes.
4. Stir in cooked quinoa and soy sauce, and cook for another 2-3 minutes.
5. Serve hot.

Baked Ziti with Spinach and Ricotta

Ingredients:

- 1 lb ziti pasta
- 1 jar marinara sauce
- 2 cups ricotta cheese
- 1 cup mozzarella cheese, shredded
- 1/2 cup Parmesan cheese, grated
- 1 bag (10 oz) frozen spinach, thawed and drained
- 1 egg
- 1 tsp garlic powder
- Salt and pepper to taste
- Fresh basil for garnish (optional)

Instructions:

1. Preheat oven to 375°F (190°C). Cook ziti pasta according to package instructions. Drain and set aside.
2. In a large bowl, combine ricotta cheese, mozzarella cheese, Parmesan, spinach, egg, garlic powder, salt, and pepper.
3. In a baking dish, spread a layer of marinara sauce, then layer with cooked ziti. Top with the ricotta and spinach mixture. Repeat layers as necessary.
4. Pour the remaining marinara sauce on top and sprinkle with extra mozzarella.
5. Bake for 25-30 minutes, or until bubbly and golden on top.
6. Garnish with fresh basil and serve hot.

Grilled Chicken with Sweet Potato Fries

Ingredients:

- 4 boneless, skinless chicken breasts
- 2 tbsp olive oil
- 1 tbsp paprika
- 1 tsp garlic powder
- 1 tsp onion powder
- Salt and pepper to taste
- 2 large sweet potatoes, peeled and cut into fries
- 1 tbsp olive oil (for fries)
- 1 tsp cinnamon
- 1 tsp paprika
- 1 tbsp fresh parsley (optional)

Instructions:

1. Preheat grill to medium-high heat.
2. In a small bowl, mix olive oil, paprika, garlic powder, onion powder, salt, and pepper. Rub this mixture over the chicken breasts.
3. Grill the chicken for 6-7 minutes per side, or until cooked through and internal temperature reaches 165°F (74°C).
4. While the chicken cooks, preheat oven to 400°F (200°C). Toss sweet potato fries with olive oil, cinnamon, paprika, salt, and pepper. Arrange on a baking sheet.
5. Bake fries for 20-25 minutes, flipping halfway through, until crispy and tender.
6. Serve grilled chicken with sweet potato fries and garnish with parsley.

Broccoli and Cheddar Stuffed Chicken

Ingredients:

- 4 boneless, skinless chicken breasts
- 1 cup broccoli florets, steamed
- 1 cup cheddar cheese, shredded
- 1/2 cup cream cheese, softened
- 1/2 tsp garlic powder
- Salt and pepper to taste
- 1 tbsp olive oil

Instructions:

1. Preheat oven to 375°F (190°C).
2. In a bowl, combine steamed broccoli, cheddar cheese, cream cheese, garlic powder, salt, and pepper. Mix well.
3. Slice each chicken breast horizontally to create a pocket. Stuff each chicken breast with the broccoli and cheese mixture.
4. Heat olive oil in a skillet over medium-high heat. Sear each chicken breast for 2-3 minutes per side until browned.
5. Transfer the chicken to the oven and bake for 15-20 minutes, or until the chicken is cooked through and the internal temperature reaches 165°F (74°C).
6. Serve hot and enjoy!

Veggie-Packed Shepherd's Pie

Ingredients:

- 1 lb ground beef or lamb
- 1 onion, chopped
- 2 garlic cloves, minced
- 2 carrots, diced
- 1 cup peas
- 1 cup corn kernels
- 2 tbsp tomato paste
- 1 cup beef or vegetable broth
- 1 tsp dried thyme
- 2 cups mashed potatoes (prepared ahead of time)
- Salt and pepper to taste

Instructions:

1. Preheat oven to 375°F (190°C).
2. In a large skillet, cook ground beef or lamb over medium heat until browned. Drain any excess fat.
3. Add onion and garlic and cook for 5 minutes, until softened.
4. Stir in carrots, peas, corn, tomato paste, broth, and thyme. Simmer for 10-15 minutes, until vegetables are tender. Season with salt and pepper.
5. Transfer the meat and vegetable mixture to a baking dish. Spread mashed potatoes on top in an even layer.
6. Bake for 20-25 minutes, or until the top is golden and bubbly.
7. Serve hot.

Grilled Salmon with Brown Rice

Ingredients:

- 4 salmon fillets
- 2 tbsp olive oil
- 1 tbsp lemon juice
- 2 garlic cloves, minced
- 1 tsp dried dill
- Salt and pepper to taste
- 2 cups cooked brown rice
- Lemon wedges for serving

Instructions:

1. Preheat grill to medium-high heat.
2. Brush the salmon fillets with olive oil, lemon juice, garlic, dill, salt, and pepper.
3. Grill the salmon for 4-6 minutes per side, or until cooked through and flakes easily with a fork.
4. Serve the grilled salmon on a bed of cooked brown rice and garnish with lemon wedges.

Beef and Vegetable Skillet

Ingredients:

- 1 lb ground beef
- 1 tbsp olive oil
- 1 onion, chopped
- 2 garlic cloves, minced
- 1 bell pepper, chopped
- 1 zucchini, sliced
- 1 cup cherry tomatoes, halved
- 1 tsp dried oregano
- Salt and pepper to taste

Instructions:

1. In a large skillet, heat olive oil over medium heat. Add ground beef and cook until browned, about 6-7 minutes.
2. Add onion and garlic, and sauté for 5 minutes until softened.
3. Stir in bell pepper, zucchini, and cherry tomatoes. Cook for an additional 5 minutes until vegetables are tender.
4. Season with oregano, salt, and pepper, and cook for another 2 minutes.
5. Serve immediately.

Sweet and Sour Chicken with Rice

Ingredients:

- 1 lb chicken breast, cut into bite-sized pieces
- 1/2 cup cornstarch
- 1 egg, beaten
- 2 tbsp vegetable oil
- 1 red bell pepper, sliced
- 1 green bell pepper, sliced
- 1 onion, sliced
- 1 can (8 oz) pineapple chunks in juice
- 1/4 cup vinegar
- 1/4 cup sugar
- 1/4 cup ketchup
- 1 tbsp soy sauce
- Cooked rice for serving

Instructions:

1. In a bowl, toss chicken pieces in cornstarch and dip in the beaten egg. Heat vegetable oil in a skillet over medium-high heat.
2. Fry the chicken in batches for 5-6 minutes, until golden brown. Remove from the skillet and set aside.
3. In the same skillet, sauté bell peppers and onion for 3-4 minutes until tender.
4. In a small bowl, mix pineapple juice, vinegar, sugar, ketchup, and soy sauce. Pour the mixture into the skillet and bring to a simmer.
5. Add fried chicken back into the skillet and stir to coat with sauce. Simmer for 5-7 minutes until heated through.
6. Serve the sweet and sour chicken over cooked rice.

Shrimp and Vegetable Skewers

Ingredients:

- 1 lb large shrimp, peeled and deveined
- 1 zucchini, sliced
- 1 bell pepper, cut into chunks
- 1 red onion, cut into chunks
- 1 tbsp olive oil
- 1 tbsp lemon juice
- 1 tsp garlic powder
- Salt and pepper to taste
- Fresh parsley for garnish

Instructions:

1. Preheat grill to medium-high heat.
2. In a bowl, toss shrimp, zucchini, bell pepper, and onion with olive oil, lemon juice, garlic powder, salt, and pepper.
3. Thread shrimp and vegetables onto skewers.
4. Grill the skewers for 2-3 minutes per side, or until shrimp is cooked through and vegetables are tender.
5. Garnish with fresh parsley and serve immediately.

Veggie and Bean Burrito Bowls

Ingredients:

- 1 cup cooked rice
- 1 can black beans, drained and rinsed
- 1 cup corn kernels (fresh or frozen)
- 1 avocado, diced
- 1/2 cup salsa
- 1/2 cup shredded cheese
- 1/2 cup sour cream
- 1/2 tsp chili powder
- 1/2 tsp cumin
- Fresh cilantro for garnish

Instructions:

1. In a bowl, mix together rice, black beans, corn, chili powder, and cumin.
2. Top the rice and bean mixture with diced avocado, salsa, shredded cheese, and sour cream.
3. Garnish with fresh cilantro and serve.

Slow-Cooker Chicken Stew

Ingredients:

- 4 boneless, skinless chicken breasts
- 4 carrots, chopped
- 3 potatoes, cubed
- 1 onion, chopped
- 2 garlic cloves, minced
- 1 cup celery, chopped
- 1 can (14.5 oz) diced tomatoes
- 4 cups chicken broth
- 1 tsp dried thyme
- 1 tsp dried rosemary
- Salt and pepper to taste
- 1/2 cup heavy cream (optional)
- Fresh parsley for garnish

Instructions:

1. Place chicken breasts, carrots, potatoes, onion, garlic, celery, diced tomatoes, and chicken broth into the slow cooker.
2. Sprinkle with thyme, rosemary, salt, and pepper. Stir to combine.
3. Cover and cook on low for 6-8 hours or on high for 4-5 hours, until the chicken and vegetables are tender.
4. Remove the chicken breasts, shred them, and return to the stew.
5. Stir in heavy cream, if using, and season to taste with salt and pepper.
6. Garnish with fresh parsley and serve.

Teriyaki Chicken with Steamed Rice

Ingredients:

- 4 boneless, skinless chicken breasts
- 1/2 cup soy sauce
- 1/4 cup honey
- 1/4 cup rice vinegar
- 2 garlic cloves, minced
- 1 tbsp ginger, grated
- 1 tbsp sesame oil
- 2 tbsp cornstarch (optional, for thickening)
- 2 cups steamed rice
- Sesame seeds and chopped green onions for garnish

Instructions:

1. In a bowl, mix together soy sauce, honey, rice vinegar, garlic, ginger, and sesame oil. Pour the marinade over the chicken breasts.
2. Marinate the chicken for at least 30 minutes or up to 4 hours in the refrigerator.
3. Preheat the grill or skillet to medium-high heat. Cook the chicken for 6-7 minutes per side until cooked through.
4. In a small saucepan, bring the marinade to a simmer over medium heat. Stir in cornstarch if you prefer a thicker sauce. Let it simmer for 2-3 minutes.
5. Serve the grilled chicken over steamed rice, drizzling with the teriyaki sauce.
6. Garnish with sesame seeds and green onions.

Beef Tacos with Fresh Salsa

Ingredients:

- 1 lb ground beef
- 1 onion, chopped
- 2 garlic cloves, minced
- 1 tbsp taco seasoning
- 1/4 cup water
- 8 small taco shells
- 1 cup shredded lettuce
- 1 cup shredded cheese
- 1/2 cup sour cream
- 1 lime, cut into wedges

Fresh Salsa:

- 2 tomatoes, chopped
- 1/2 onion, finely chopped
- 1 jalapeño, seeded and minced
- 1/4 cup cilantro, chopped
- 1 tbsp lime juice
- Salt and pepper to taste

Instructions:

1. In a skillet, cook ground beef over medium heat until browned, breaking it apart as it cooks. Drain any excess fat.
2. Add chopped onion and garlic, cooking until softened, about 3 minutes. Stir in taco seasoning and water, simmering for 5 minutes.
3. To make the salsa, combine tomatoes, onion, jalapeño, cilantro, lime juice, salt, and pepper in a bowl. Set aside.
4. Warm taco shells in the oven according to package instructions.
5. Fill each taco shell with beef mixture, shredded lettuce, cheese, and a dollop of sour cream.
6. Top with fresh salsa and serve with lime wedges.

Turkey and Sweet Potato Chili

Ingredients:

- 1 lb ground turkey
- 1 onion, chopped
- 2 garlic cloves, minced
- 2 sweet potatoes, peeled and cubed
- 1 can (14.5 oz) diced tomatoes
- 1 can (15 oz) kidney beans, drained and rinsed
- 1 can (15 oz) black beans, drained and rinsed
- 1 tbsp chili powder
- 1 tsp cumin
- 1/2 tsp smoked paprika
- Salt and pepper to taste
- 4 cups chicken broth
- 1 tbsp olive oil
- Fresh cilantro for garnish

Instructions:

1. Heat olive oil in a large pot over medium heat. Add ground turkey, cooking until browned.
2. Add onion and garlic, sautéing until softened, about 5 minutes.
3. Stir in sweet potatoes, diced tomatoes, beans, chili powder, cumin, paprika, salt, and pepper.
4. Add chicken broth and bring to a simmer. Let it cook for 25-30 minutes, until sweet potatoes are tender.
5. Adjust seasoning if necessary, and garnish with fresh cilantro before serving.

Creamy Vegetable Soup with Whole Wheat Croutons

Ingredients:

- 1 tbsp olive oil
- 1 onion, chopped
- 2 garlic cloves, minced
- 2 carrots, chopped
- 2 potatoes, peeled and cubed
- 1 zucchini, chopped
- 1 cup green beans, chopped
- 4 cups vegetable broth
- 1 cup heavy cream
- Salt and pepper to taste

Whole Wheat Croutons:

- 2 cups cubed whole wheat bread
- 2 tbsp olive oil
- 1 tsp garlic powder
- 1 tsp dried oregano
- Salt to taste

Instructions:

1. Heat olive oil in a large pot. Add onion and garlic, cooking until softened, about 5 minutes.
2. Add carrots, potatoes, zucchini, and green beans. Stir in vegetable broth and bring to a simmer.
3. Let the soup cook for 25-30 minutes, or until vegetables are tender.
4. Stir in heavy cream and season with salt and pepper.
5. For the croutons, preheat the oven to 375°F (190°C). Toss cubed bread with olive oil, garlic powder, oregano, and salt.
6. Bake for 10-15 minutes, turning once, until crispy and golden.
7. Serve the soup hot, topped with whole wheat croutons.

Grilled Pork Chops with Apple Slaw

Ingredients:

- 4 boneless pork chops
- 1 tbsp olive oil
- 1 tsp paprika
- 1 tsp garlic powder
- Salt and pepper to taste

Apple Slaw:

- 2 apples, julienned
- 1 cup shredded cabbage
- 1/2 cup shredded carrots
- 2 tbsp apple cider vinegar
- 1 tbsp honey
- Salt and pepper to taste

Instructions:

1. Preheat the grill to medium-high heat.
2. Rub pork chops with olive oil, paprika, garlic powder, salt, and pepper. Grill for 4-5 minutes per side until cooked through.
3. For the slaw, toss apples, cabbage, and carrots in a bowl. In a separate small bowl, whisk together apple cider vinegar, honey, salt, and pepper. Pour over the slaw and toss to combine.
4. Serve the grilled pork chops with apple slaw on the side.

Lemon Herb Chicken with Quinoa

Ingredients:

- 4 boneless, skinless chicken breasts
- 1 tbsp olive oil
- 1 lemon, zest and juice
- 2 garlic cloves, minced
- 1 tsp dried thyme
- 1 tsp dried rosemary
- Salt and pepper to taste
- 1 cup quinoa
- 2 cups chicken broth

Instructions:

1. Preheat grill or skillet to medium-high heat.
2. Rub chicken breasts with olive oil, lemon zest, lemon juice, garlic, thyme, rosemary, salt, and pepper.
3. Grill the chicken for 6-7 minutes per side until fully cooked.
4. Meanwhile, cook quinoa: rinse the quinoa and combine it with chicken broth in a pot. Bring to a boil, then reduce to a simmer and cover. Cook for 15-20 minutes until the liquid is absorbed.
5. Serve the grilled chicken over quinoa, with a wedge of lemon for garnish.

Baked Salmon with Avocado Salsa

Ingredients:

- 4 salmon fillets
- 1 tbsp olive oil
- Salt and pepper to taste
- 1 tsp paprika

Avocado Salsa:

- 2 ripe avocados, diced
- 1 small red onion, chopped
- 1 cup cherry tomatoes, halved
- 1 tbsp lime juice
- 2 tbsp cilantro, chopped
- Salt and pepper to taste

Instructions:

1. Preheat oven to 375°F (190°C). Place salmon fillets on a baking sheet, drizzle with olive oil, and sprinkle with salt, pepper, and paprika.
2. Bake for 12-15 minutes, or until salmon flakes easily with a fork.
3. For the salsa, combine avocado, onion, tomatoes, lime juice, cilantro, salt, and pepper in a bowl.
4. Serve the baked salmon topped with avocado salsa.

Roasted Veggie Buddha Bowls

Ingredients:

- 1 sweet potato, peeled and cubed
- 1 cup broccoli florets
- 1 red bell pepper, sliced
- 1 tbsp olive oil
- 1 tsp smoked paprika
- Salt and pepper to taste
- 1 cup cooked quinoa
- 1/4 cup tahini
- 2 tbsp lemon juice
- 1 tbsp olive oil
- 1 tbsp water
- Fresh parsley for garnish

Instructions:

1. Preheat oven to 400°F (200°C).
2. Toss sweet potato, broccoli, and bell pepper with olive oil, paprika, salt, and pepper. Roast for 25-30 minutes, flipping halfway through.
3. While the veggies roast, prepare the quinoa according to package instructions.
4. Whisk together tahini, lemon juice, olive oil, and water to make the dressing.
5. Assemble the bowls: Divide quinoa among bowls, top with roasted veggies, and drizzle with tahini dressing.
6. Garnish with fresh parsley.

Spaghetti Squash Primavera

Ingredients:

- 1 medium spaghetti squash
- 1 tbsp olive oil
- 1 onion, sliced
- 2 garlic cloves, minced
- 1 bell pepper, chopped
- 1 zucchini, sliced
- 1 cup cherry tomatoes, halved
- 1/2 cup fresh basil, chopped
- 1/4 cup grated Parmesan cheese
- Salt and pepper to taste

Instructions:

1. Preheat the oven to 400°F (200°C). Cut the spaghetti squash in half lengthwise and scoop out the seeds. Drizzle with olive oil, salt, and pepper, then place cut-side down on a baking sheet. Roast for 35-40 minutes, or until tender.
2. While the squash roasts, heat olive oil in a skillet over medium heat. Add onion and garlic, sautéing for 2-3 minutes.
3. Add bell pepper, zucchini, and cherry tomatoes to the skillet. Cook for 5-7 minutes, until vegetables are tender.
4. Once the spaghetti squash is done, use a fork to scrape out the strands. Toss the strands with the sautéed vegetables, fresh basil, and Parmesan cheese.
5. Season with salt and pepper, and serve immediately.

Chicken Fajitas with Peppers and Onions

Ingredients:

- 1 lb boneless, skinless chicken breasts, sliced
- 1 red bell pepper, sliced
- 1 green bell pepper, sliced
- 1 onion, sliced
- 2 tbsp olive oil
- 2 tsp chili powder
- 1 tsp cumin
- 1 tsp paprika
- 1/2 tsp garlic powder
- Salt and pepper to taste
- 8 small tortillas
- Fresh cilantro for garnish
- Lime wedges for serving

Instructions:

1. In a large skillet, heat olive oil over medium heat. Add the chicken and cook for 5-7 minutes, until browned and cooked through. Remove from the skillet and set aside.
2. In the same skillet, add the bell peppers and onion. Cook for 5-6 minutes, stirring occasionally, until softened.
3. Return the chicken to the skillet. Sprinkle with chili powder, cumin, paprika, garlic powder, salt, and pepper. Stir to combine and cook for another 2-3 minutes.
4. Serve the fajita mixture in tortillas, garnished with cilantro and lime wedges.

Mediterranean Chicken with Hummus and Veggies

Ingredients:

- 4 boneless, skinless chicken breasts
- 1 tbsp olive oil
- 1 tsp dried oregano
- 1 tsp garlic powder
- 1/2 tsp cumin
- Salt and pepper to taste
- 1 cup hummus
- 1 cucumber, sliced
- 1 tomato, chopped
- 1/4 red onion, thinly sliced
- 1/4 cup Kalamata olives, pitted and sliced
- Fresh parsley for garnish

Instructions:

1. Preheat the grill or skillet to medium-high heat. Season the chicken breasts with olive oil, oregano, garlic powder, cumin, salt, and pepper.
2. Grill the chicken for 6-7 minutes per side, until cooked through.
3. While the chicken is cooking, prepare the veggies. Toss cucumber, tomato, red onion, and olives together in a bowl.
4. Serve the chicken with a side of hummus, and garnish with fresh parsley. Top with the veggie mixture.

Beef and Sweet Potato Stir-Fry

Ingredients:

- 1 lb beef sirloin, thinly sliced
- 2 medium sweet potatoes, peeled and cubed
- 1 tbsp olive oil
- 1 onion, sliced
- 2 garlic cloves, minced
- 1 bell pepper, sliced
- 2 tbsp soy sauce
- 1 tbsp honey
- 1 tsp ground ginger
- 1/2 tsp red pepper flakes (optional)
- Salt and pepper to taste

Instructions:

1. In a large skillet or wok, heat olive oil over medium-high heat. Add the sweet potato cubes and cook for 8-10 minutes, until tender. Remove from the skillet and set aside.
2. In the same skillet, add the sliced beef. Cook for 3-5 minutes, until browned and cooked through. Remove from the skillet and set aside.
3. Add onion, garlic, and bell pepper to the skillet, sautéing for 3-4 minutes until softened.
4. Stir in soy sauce, honey, ground ginger, and red pepper flakes. Return the beef and sweet potatoes to the skillet and toss to combine.
5. Cook for another 2-3 minutes, allowing the sauce to thicken. Serve hot.

Veggie-Loaded Pasta Primavera

Ingredients:

- 8 oz whole wheat pasta
- 1 tbsp olive oil
- 1 onion, chopped
- 2 garlic cloves, minced
- 1 zucchini, sliced
- 1 bell pepper, chopped
- 1 cup cherry tomatoes, halved
- 1/2 cup peas
- 1/4 cup Parmesan cheese, grated
- Fresh basil for garnish
- Salt and pepper to taste

Instructions:

1. Cook the pasta according to package instructions. Drain and set aside.
2. In a large skillet, heat olive oil over medium heat. Add onion and garlic, cooking until softened, about 3 minutes.
3. Add zucchini, bell pepper, cherry tomatoes, and peas. Cook for 5-7 minutes until vegetables are tender.
4. Toss the cooked pasta with the sautéed vegetables. Stir in Parmesan cheese and season with salt and pepper.
5. Garnish with fresh basil and serve.

Chicken and Broccoli Casserole

Ingredients:

- 2 cups cooked chicken, shredded
- 4 cups broccoli florets, steamed
- 1 can (10.5 oz) cream of chicken soup
- 1/2 cup Greek yogurt
- 1/2 cup shredded cheddar cheese
- 1/4 cup breadcrumbs
- 1 tbsp olive oil
- Salt and pepper to taste

Instructions:

1. Preheat the oven to 375°F (190°C). Lightly grease a casserole dish.
2. In a large bowl, combine shredded chicken, steamed broccoli, cream of chicken soup, Greek yogurt, and shredded cheddar cheese. Stir to combine.
3. Transfer the mixture to the casserole dish. Top with breadcrumbs and drizzle with olive oil.
4. Bake for 20-25 minutes, until bubbly and golden brown on top.
5. Season with salt and pepper, and serve.

Grilled Steak with Mashed Cauliflower

Ingredients:

- 2 steaks (your choice of cut)
- 1 tbsp olive oil
- 1 tsp garlic powder
- Salt and pepper to taste
- 1 head cauliflower, chopped
- 2 tbsp butter
- 1/4 cup milk
- Fresh parsley for garnish

Instructions:

1. Preheat the grill or skillet to medium-high heat. Rub the steaks with olive oil, garlic powder, salt, and pepper.
2. Grill the steaks for 4-6 minutes per side, depending on desired doneness.
3. While the steaks cook, steam the cauliflower until tender, about 10 minutes.
4. Mash the cauliflower with butter and milk, seasoning with salt and pepper.
5. Serve the steaks with mashed cauliflower and garnish with fresh parsley.

Veggie-Packed Baked Mac and Cheese

Ingredients:

- 8 oz elbow macaroni
- 2 cups broccoli florets, steamed
- 1 cup shredded cheddar cheese
- 1 cup shredded mozzarella cheese
- 2 cups milk
- 1 tbsp butter
- 2 tbsp flour
- 1 tsp garlic powder
- Salt and pepper to taste
- 1/2 cup breadcrumbs

Instructions:

1. Preheat the oven to 350°F (175°C). Cook the macaroni according to package instructions. Drain and set aside.
2. In a saucepan, melt butter over medium heat. Stir in flour and garlic powder to form a roux. Gradually whisk in the milk and cook until the sauce thickens, about 5 minutes.
3. Stir in shredded cheeses until melted and smooth. Season with salt and pepper.
4. In a large bowl, combine the cooked macaroni, steamed broccoli, and cheese sauce. Pour into a greased baking dish.
5. Top with breadcrumbs and bake for 15-20 minutes, until golden and bubbly.
6. Serve hot.

Slow-Cooker Beef and Vegetable Soup

Ingredients:

- 1 lb beef stew meat
- 4 cups beef broth
- 1 onion, chopped
- 2 carrots, sliced
- 2 potatoes, cubed
- 1 cup green beans, chopped
- 1 can (14.5 oz) diced tomatoes
- 2 garlic cloves, minced
- 1 tsp dried thyme
- Salt and pepper to taste

Instructions:

1. In a slow cooker, combine beef stew meat, beef broth, onion, carrots, potatoes, green beans, diced tomatoes, garlic, thyme, salt, and pepper.
2. Stir to combine. Cover and cook on low for 7-8 hours or on high for 4 hours, until the beef is tender.
3. Taste and adjust seasoning if needed. Serve hot.

Fish Tacos with Mango Salsa

Ingredients:

- 4 fish fillets (such as tilapia or cod)
- 1 tbsp olive oil
- 1 tsp chili powder
- 1/2 tsp cumin
- Salt and pepper to taste
- 8 small tortillas
- 1 mango, peeled and diced
- 1/4 cup red onion, finely chopped
- 1/4 cup fresh cilantro, chopped
- 1 lime, juiced

Instructions:

1. Preheat a grill or skillet over medium heat. Rub the fish fillets with olive oil, chili powder, cumin, salt, and pepper.
2. Grill or cook the fish for 3-4 minutes per side, until cooked through and flaky.
3. While the fish cooks, prepare the salsa by combining mango, red onion, cilantro, and lime juice in a bowl.
4. Assemble the tacos by placing fish fillets in tortillas and topping with mango salsa.
5. Serve with lime wedges.

One-Pan Baked Chicken and Veggies

Ingredients:

- 4 bone-in, skinless chicken thighs
- 2 cups baby potatoes, halved
- 1 cup carrots, sliced
- 1 red bell pepper, chopped
- 1 onion, sliced
- 3 tbsp olive oil
- 2 tsp garlic powder
- 1 tsp paprika
- Salt and pepper to taste
- Fresh parsley for garnish

Instructions:

1. Preheat the oven to 400°F (200°C). Line a large baking sheet with parchment paper or lightly grease it.
2. Arrange the chicken thighs in the center of the baking sheet. Surround with baby potatoes, carrots, bell pepper, and onion.
3. Drizzle everything with olive oil, and sprinkle with garlic powder, paprika, salt, and pepper. Toss the veggies to coat evenly.
4. Bake for 35-40 minutes, or until the chicken is cooked through and the vegetables are tender.
5. Garnish with fresh parsley and serve.

Roasted Turkey with Cranberry Sauce

Ingredients:

- 1 whole turkey (about 10-12 lbs)
- 1/4 cup olive oil
- 1 tbsp rosemary, chopped
- 1 tbsp thyme, chopped
- Salt and pepper to taste
- 2 cups low-sodium chicken broth
- 1 tbsp butter

For the Cranberry Sauce:

- 1 cup fresh cranberries
- 1/2 cup sugar
- 1/2 cup water
- 1 tbsp orange zest
- 1 tsp cinnamon

Instructions:

1. Preheat the oven to 325°F (165°C). Pat the turkey dry with paper towels.
2. Rub the turkey with olive oil, rosemary, thyme, salt, and pepper. Place it in a roasting pan and pour chicken broth around the turkey.
3. Roast for 2-3 hours, basting occasionally, until the internal temperature reaches 165°F (74°C).
4. For the cranberry sauce, combine cranberries, sugar, water, orange zest, and cinnamon in a saucepan. Bring to a boil, then simmer for 15-20 minutes, until thickened.
5. Let the turkey rest for 15 minutes before carving. Serve with cranberry sauce.

Pesto Chicken and Zucchini Noodles

Ingredients:

- 4 boneless, skinless chicken breasts
- 2 tbsp olive oil
- 2 zucchini, spiralized into noodles
- 1/2 cup pesto sauce (store-bought or homemade)
- Salt and pepper to taste
- Fresh Parmesan cheese for garnish

Instructions:

1. Heat olive oil in a large skillet over medium heat. Season the chicken breasts with salt and pepper, then cook for 6-7 minutes per side, until cooked through.
2. Remove the chicken from the skillet and set aside. In the same skillet, add zucchini noodles and cook for 2-3 minutes until tender.
3. Toss the zucchini noodles with pesto sauce, and serve with the chicken on top.
4. Garnish with fresh Parmesan cheese and serve immediately.

Eggplant Parmesan with Spaghetti

Ingredients:

- 2 large eggplants, sliced into 1/2-inch rounds
- 2 cups breadcrumbs
- 1/2 cup grated Parmesan cheese
- 2 cups marinara sauce
- 2 cups shredded mozzarella cheese
- 1 egg, beaten
- 2 tbsp olive oil
- Salt and pepper to taste
- 8 oz spaghetti, cooked

Instructions:

1. Preheat the oven to 375°F (190°C). Place breadcrumbs and Parmesan cheese in a shallow bowl. Dip eggplant slices in the beaten egg, then coat in the breadcrumb mixture.
2. Heat olive oil in a skillet over medium heat. Fry the eggplant slices for 2-3 minutes on each side, until golden brown. Transfer to a paper towel-lined plate.
3. In a baking dish, spread a layer of marinara sauce. Layer eggplant slices on top, followed by mozzarella cheese. Repeat the layers.
4. Bake for 20-25 minutes, until the cheese is melted and bubbly. Serve with spaghetti.

BBQ Chicken with Roasted Potatoes

Ingredients:

- 4 boneless, skinless chicken breasts
- 1/2 cup BBQ sauce
- 2 tbsp olive oil
- 1 lb baby potatoes, halved
- 1 tsp paprika
- Salt and pepper to taste
- Fresh cilantro for garnish

Instructions:

1. Preheat the oven to 400°F (200°C). Line a baking sheet with parchment paper.
2. In a large bowl, toss the baby potatoes with olive oil, paprika, salt, and pepper. Spread them out in a single layer on the baking sheet.
3. Place the chicken breasts on another baking sheet and brush with BBQ sauce.
4. Roast the potatoes and chicken in the oven for 25-30 minutes, until the chicken reaches an internal temperature of 165°F (74°C) and the potatoes are tender.
5. Garnish with fresh cilantro and serve with extra BBQ sauce.

Sweet Potato and Black Bean Enchiladas

Ingredients:

- 2 large sweet potatoes, peeled and diced
- 1 tbsp olive oil
- 1 can (15 oz) black beans, drained and rinsed
- 1 cup enchilada sauce
- 8 small flour tortillas
- 1 cup shredded cheese (cheddar or Mexican blend)
- 1/2 tsp cumin
- 1/2 tsp chili powder
- Salt and pepper to taste
- Fresh cilantro for garnish

Instructions:

1. Preheat the oven to 375°F (190°C). Toss the diced sweet potatoes with olive oil, cumin, chili powder, salt, and pepper. Roast for 20-25 minutes, until tender.
2. In a bowl, combine the roasted sweet potatoes, black beans, and half of the cheese.
3. Spoon the mixture onto the center of each tortilla, roll up, and place seam-side down in a baking dish.
4. Pour enchilada sauce over the top of the rolled tortillas, and sprinkle with the remaining cheese.
5. Bake for 20 minutes, until the cheese is melted and bubbly. Garnish with fresh cilantro and serve.

Grilled Chicken Caesar Salad

Ingredients:

- 4 boneless, skinless chicken breasts
- 1 tbsp olive oil
- Salt and pepper to taste
- 6 cups Romaine lettuce, chopped
- 1/2 cup Caesar dressing
- 1/4 cup grated Parmesan cheese
- 1/2 cup croutons
- 1 lemon, cut into wedges

Instructions:

1. Preheat the grill to medium-high heat. Brush the chicken breasts with olive oil and season with salt and pepper.
2. Grill the chicken for 6-7 minutes on each side, or until fully cooked and the internal temperature reaches 165°F (74°C).
3. Let the chicken rest for a few minutes, then slice into strips.
4. In a large bowl, toss the lettuce with Caesar dressing. Top with sliced chicken, grated Parmesan, croutons, and lemon wedges.
5. Serve immediately and enjoy!

Baked Falafel with Couscous

Ingredients:

- 1 can (15 oz) chickpeas, drained and rinsed
- 1/4 cup fresh parsley, chopped
- 1/4 cup fresh cilantro, chopped
- 1 small onion, chopped
- 2 garlic cloves, minced
- 1 tsp ground cumin
- 1/2 tsp ground coriander
- 1/2 tsp baking powder
- 1/4 cup whole wheat flour
- Salt and pepper to taste
- 2 tbsp olive oil
- 1 cup couscous
- 1 1/2 cups water

Instructions:

1. Preheat the oven to 375°F (190°C). Line a baking sheet with parchment paper.
2. In a food processor, combine chickpeas, parsley, cilantro, onion, garlic, cumin, coriander, baking powder, flour, salt, and pepper. Pulse until a thick dough forms.
3. Shape the dough into small balls and place them on the prepared baking sheet. Drizzle with olive oil.
4. Bake for 25-30 minutes, flipping halfway through, until golden and crispy.
5. Meanwhile, bring water to a boil in a saucepan, then stir in couscous. Cover and remove from heat. Let it steam for 5 minutes, then fluff with a fork.
6. Serve the falafel on top of couscous and enjoy!

Stuffed Bell Peppers with Brown Rice

Ingredients:

- 4 bell peppers, tops cut off and seeds removed
- 1 cup cooked brown rice
- 1 lb ground turkey or beef
- 1 can (15 oz) diced tomatoes, drained
- 1 small onion, chopped
- 1 tsp garlic powder
- 1 tsp dried oregano
- 1/2 cup shredded cheese (optional)
- Salt and pepper to taste

Instructions:

1. Preheat the oven to 375°F (190°C). Place the bell peppers in a baking dish.
2. In a large skillet, cook the ground turkey or beef over medium heat until browned, about 6-8 minutes. Drain any excess fat.
3. Add the cooked brown rice, diced tomatoes, onion, garlic powder, oregano, salt, and pepper to the skillet. Stir to combine.
4. Stuff the bell peppers with the rice mixture and top with shredded cheese, if using.
5. Cover the dish with foil and bake for 25-30 minutes, until the peppers are tender.
6. Serve and enjoy!

Turkey Burgers with Avocado

Ingredients:

- 1 lb ground turkey
- 1/4 cup breadcrumbs
- 1 egg
- 1 tbsp Worcestershire sauce
- Salt and pepper to taste
- 1 avocado, sliced
- 4 whole wheat burger buns
- Lettuce and tomato for garnish

Instructions:

1. In a bowl, combine ground turkey, breadcrumbs, egg, Worcestershire sauce, salt, and pepper. Mix well.
2. Shape the mixture into 4 patties.
3. Heat a grill or skillet over medium heat. Cook the turkey burgers for 5-7 minutes per side, or until the internal temperature reaches 165°F (74°C).
4. Toast the burger buns and assemble the burgers with the turkey patties, avocado slices, lettuce, and tomato.
5. Serve immediately and enjoy!

Beef and Barley Soup

Ingredients:

- 1 lb beef stew meat, cubed
- 2 tbsp olive oil
- 1 onion, chopped
- 2 carrots, sliced
- 2 celery stalks, chopped
- 2 garlic cloves, minced
- 6 cups beef broth
- 1 cup pearl barley
- 1 tsp dried thyme
- Salt and pepper to taste
- Fresh parsley for garnish

Instructions:

1. Heat olive oil in a large pot over medium heat. Brown the beef stew meat on all sides, then remove from the pot and set aside.
2. In the same pot, sauté the onion, carrots, celery, and garlic for 5 minutes, until softened.
3. Add the beef broth, pearl barley, thyme, salt, and pepper. Bring to a boil.
4. Reduce the heat and simmer for 45 minutes, or until the barley and beef are tender.
5. Garnish with fresh parsley and serve.

Shrimp Scampi with Whole Wheat Pasta

Ingredients:

- 1 lb shrimp, peeled and deveined
- 8 oz whole wheat pasta
- 4 tbsp olive oil
- 4 garlic cloves, minced
- 1/2 tsp red pepper flakes
- 1/2 cup white wine (or chicken broth)
- 1/4 cup fresh lemon juice
- 1/4 cup chopped fresh parsley
- Salt and pepper to taste

Instructions:

1. Cook the whole wheat pasta according to package instructions. Drain and set aside.
2. In a large skillet, heat olive oil over medium heat. Add garlic and red pepper flakes, and sauté for 1-2 minutes.
3. Add the shrimp and cook for 3-4 minutes, until pink and cooked through.
4. Pour in the white wine (or chicken broth) and lemon juice. Stir to combine and let it simmer for 2-3 minutes.
5. Toss the cooked pasta into the skillet with the shrimp. Stir in fresh parsley, salt, and pepper.
6. Serve immediately and enjoy!

Chicken and Spinach Quesadillas

Ingredients:

- 2 cups cooked chicken, shredded
- 2 cups fresh spinach, chopped
- 1 cup shredded cheese (cheddar or Mexican blend)
- 4 large flour tortillas
- 1 tbsp olive oil
- Salsa for serving

Instructions:

1. In a bowl, combine the shredded chicken, chopped spinach, and shredded cheese.
2. Heat a skillet over medium heat and lightly brush with olive oil.
3. Place one tortilla in the skillet, then spoon some of the chicken and spinach mixture onto one half. Fold the tortilla in half.
4. Cook for 3-4 minutes on each side, until golden brown and the cheese is melted.
5. Repeat with the remaining tortillas and serve with salsa.